# Exploring *The* BUILDING BLOCKS *of* SCIENCE

## Book 2

### STUDENT TEXTBOOK

# REBECCA W. KELLER, PhD

Illustrations:   Janet Moneymaker
Editor:          Marjie Bassler

Exploring the Building Blocks of Science Book 2 Student Textbook (hardcover)

ISBN  978-1-936114-33-7

Published by Gravitas Publications, Inc.
Real Science-4-Kids®
www.realscience4kids.com
www.gravitaspublications.com

# Contents

## Introduction

## Chemistry

# Biology

# Physics

# Astronomy

# Conclusion

# Chapter 1  The Tools of Science

# 1.1 Introduction

How do scientists study the world around them? How do they know how fast an electron travels or what the back of a butterfly wing looks like? How do they see faraway planets or measure the size of an earthquake?

Scientists use basic and advanced tools (instruments) to measure, weigh, calculate, and explore the world around them. An advanced scientific tool, or instrument, is a tool that is more complicated than a basic tool and is used to do detailed and exact work. Basic tools and instruments help scientists crack open rocks, magnify small animals, and measure air temperatures.

Tools are a very important part of doing science. Without basic and advanced tools, scientists would not be able to cure diseases and create new materials, and they would not have been able to invent computers!

# 1.2 Brief History

Both basic and advanced tools began as inventions that helped people control and understand their surroundings. An invention is something new that someone creates to help them do a certain task.

For example, if there were no ladders, you might find it hard to get apples from the top of a tree. This might lead you to think about different ways you could get the apples. If you rolled a nearby boulder over to the tree, you might be able stand on it to reach the branches. Or you might think of using ropes to pull yourself up. By thinking about ways to reach the apples and experimenting with your ideas, you are "inventing" ways solve the problem.

The same thing happens when scientists invent tools to help them study the world around them. They think of tools that might allow them to see details better, hear sounds better, or sense temperatures better. Then they create the tools that will help them make these kinds of observations.

Tool making has a very long history. Many historians think the first tools that people invented were those used in controlling water so food could be grown. The ancient land of Mesopotamia, located between the Tigris and Euphrates rivers, was one area where tools were used to bring water to farms. (This area is now the country of Iraq.) Early farmers in Mesopotamia used walls and channels to guide water into fields to grow food. The early Egyptians and Chinese used dams, canals, and artificial lakes to control water for growing food.

Because ancient people were always testing new ways to make their living conditions better, the tools they invented were continually improved upon and adapted. With these new tools, ancient people were able to explore better ways to grow food, how to build taller buildings, and how to use metals for weapons. Ancient people also developed tools for making beautiful sculptures, glass objects, pottery, and wooden furniture.

It is hard to pinpoint exactly when and where the first instruments were used, but instruments also began in simple forms that were improved on over time. The advanced scientific instruments of today make it possible for scientists

to understand and explore more and more of the world around us. Advanced scientific instruments allow scientists to explore very small things, such as atoms, and also very big things, such as the Sun.

# 1.3 Basic Tools

The most important tools scientists use are their own five senses—sight, hearing, smell, touch, and taste. To explore the

world around them, scientists make many observations by using just their five senses. For example, scientists can observe the size of an elephant and the color of a frog. Scientists can observe that a car travels faster than a snail and that stars shine in the night sky.

However, there is a limit to how much information the five senses can provide. Basic tools extend the senses. By using basic tools, scientists can make objects appear larger, measure liquids more accurately, and determine the temperature of a body of water. Some basic tools include magnifying lenses, thermometers, beakers, and hammers.

With these basic tools, scientists can explore temperature, how ants carry food to their homes, and what minerals are inside a rock or geode. Basic tools are easy to use, and many are light and small enough to carry in a backpack.

# 1.4 Advanced Tools

Basic tools can only go so far in providing information to scientists. A magnifying glass is great for observing ants, but it won't work to see the cells inside the ant. A thermometer is great for measuring the temperature of a pond, but it can't measure the temperature of a faraway star. A hammer is perfect for opening up a rock and exposing the crystals, but it can't open up the crystals to expose the atoms.

In order to observe cells, measure the temperature of stars, or see atoms, more advanced tools are needed. An instrument is an advanced tool that allows scientists to do things such as take more precise measurements or collect more detailed data.

For example, as a scientist you might want to know exactly how much a tiny sample of salt weighs. To measure the weight, you would use a scale of some sort. In general, a basic scale won't work with a tiny amount, so you would need to use a more advanced analytical scale. Maybe you are doing an experiment with electricity and need to find out how many electrons are traveling through wires. To do this you would need to use a voltmeter to measure the flow of electrons. Or maybe you want to see how many atoms are on the surface of a piece of carbon. You would use a scanning tunneling microscope to see the atoms you want to count.

These and many other instruments help scientists measure, weigh, and observe features that can't be observed with basic tools or their own five senses.

# 1.5 Summary

- Basic and advanced tools help scientists explore the world around them.

- Ancient people started to use tools to control water and grow food.

- Basic tools extend the five senses—sight, hearing, smell, touch, and taste.

- Advanced scientific tools (instruments) help scientists observe features that basic tools cannot.

# Chapter 2   Chemist's Toolbox

## 2.1 Introduction

How do you study tiny atoms? How do you see small molecules? How can you measure, weigh, and monitor chemical reactions?

Today, chemists use a variety of tools to study atoms, molecules, and chemical reactions. The tools chemists use include special types of glass, metals, and equipment to study the smallest building blocks of matter. In this chapter we will take a look at some of these tools.

## 2.2 Brief History

The earliest chemists were called alchemists. Alchemists tried very hard to turn metals, such as lead, into gold. They never got it to work, but they did learn about chemical reactions. Alchemists were not true chemists as we know them today, because alchemists did not use a scientific method. But alchemists learned a great deal about how different chemicals react with other chemicals.

Early chemistry tools and equipment used by alchemists were made of glass, clay, stone, and a variety of metals. One early chemistry tool called the alembic was used by early Greek and Arabic alchemists to make perfumes and medicines. Another early chemistry tool called the pelican was similar to the

alembic and was also used to purify materials for medicines, perfumes, and alcohol. Today, alembics and pelicans continue to be important tools in chemistry labs.

# 2.3 Basic Chemistry Tools

Chemists use many different kinds of tools and equipment. Most chemistry labs have both basic tools and advanced tools (instruments).

Chemists often need to measure the quantity of a liquid. A liquid is any pourable substance, such as water. You can't measure liquid water with a ruler, so you have to put it into a container that will help you measure how much you have.

For example, when you bake a cake, you use a measuring cup to measure liquids such as water, milk, and vegetable oil. A chemist uses a basic tool called a beaker in the same way as you use a measuring cup. Like a measuring cup, a beaker has lines on it showing how much liquid it contains, and it has a small spout

Beaker

for pouring. Beakers don't have a handle like a measuring cup, and the sides of beakers are straight up and down rather than being angled. In a chemistry lab, a beaker does the same job as a measuring cup.

Simple scales and balances are basic tools found in chemistry labs. To measure how much "stuff" there is, scales and balances are used. To find out how much of you there is, you would use a scale. When you go to the doctor's office, they have you step on a platform. They adjust some weights to show how much you weigh, or they read a number from a display. A scale is used to weigh you, just like a chemist uses a scale to weigh objects in the lab!

# 2.4 Advanced Chemistry Tools

All over the world there are many different types of chemistry labs studying different kinds of chemistry. Often you can find advanced tools (instruments) in these labs.

For example, a lab that is studying gases might use a gas chromatograph. A gas chromatograph is an instrument that can detect different types of gases in even very small amounts. A gas chromatograph has long tubes connected to a computer or a machine that draws graphs. The chemist puts a gas in one of the tubes, the gas chromatograph tests it, and the results are displayed on a computer or are printed out.

Many chemistry labs research ways to make new chemicals. Some of their experiments are quite complicated. For example, sometimes a chemistry experiment might require that little or no oxygen gas come in contact with the chemicals, so specialized equipment is used to keep the oxygen out. These experiments require advanced glassware of different sizes and shapes. Like the alembic and pelican, some of this glassware has funny names, such as an Erlenmeyer bulb or a Buchner flask!

It is not uncommon for chemists to make their own specialized tubes and glassware to use in specific experiments. In school, many young chemists learn how to blow, cut, and mold glass so they can create unique glassware for special experiments.

# 2.5 Summary

○ Chemists use a variety of basic tools and specialized advanced instruments to do experiments.

○ The early alchemists tried to turn lead into gold.

○ Some basic chemistry tools are beakers, scales, and balances.

○ Chemists sometimes make their own specialized glassware to use in experiments.

# Chapter 3    Acids and Bases

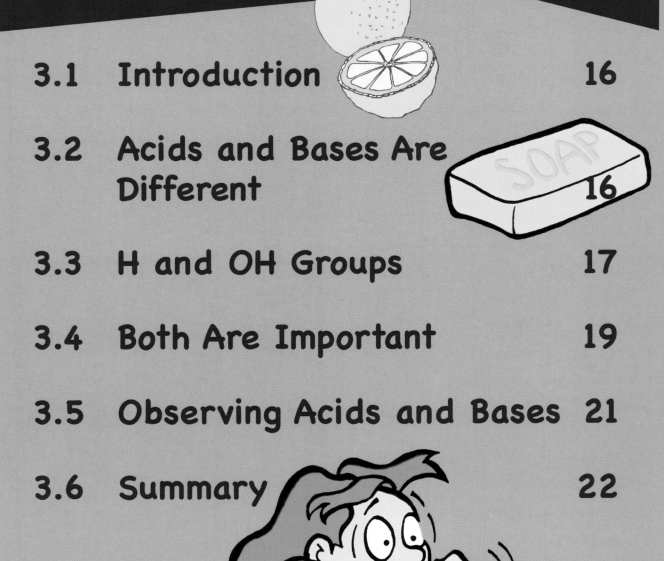

Chemistry

# 3.1 Introduction

When atoms and molecules meet, they can trade places, join together, or separate from each other. A chemical reaction happens when atoms or molecules meet and any of these changes take place. A chemical reaction is one of the events chemists measure with tools.

In this chapter we will look at some special kinds of chemical reactions. These reactions are called acid-base reactions. Acid-base reactions are easy for chemists to study with some basic tools.

# 3.2 Acids and Bases Are Different

Have you ever noticed that when you bite a lemon it tastes sour and makes your cheeks pucker?

Have you ever tasted mineral water or baking soda water? They are not sour like a lemon. They are bitter or salty.

Have you ever noticed that soap is very slippery in your fingers, but lemon juice and vinegar are not?

The molecules inside a lemon are different from the molecules inside baking soda water or mineral water. Lemons have molecules in them called acids. It is the acid in lemons that gives them their sour taste.

Baking soda water and soap contain molecules that are called bases. Bases often make things feel slippery or taste bitter.

# 3.3 H and OH Groups

Acids and bases are different from each other in many ways. This is because a base is a different kind of molecule than an acid. Acids and bases are different because they have different atom groups.

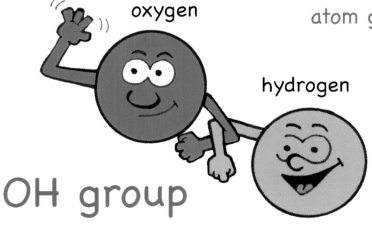

oxygen

hydrogen

OH group

A base has an OH group [say "O" "H" group]. An OH group is just an oxygen atom and a hydrogen atom together.

Most common acids have an H group [say "H" group]. An H group is just a hydrogen atom.

We can see in the next picture that sodium hydroxide (a base) has an OH group and hydrogen chloride (an acid) has an H group.

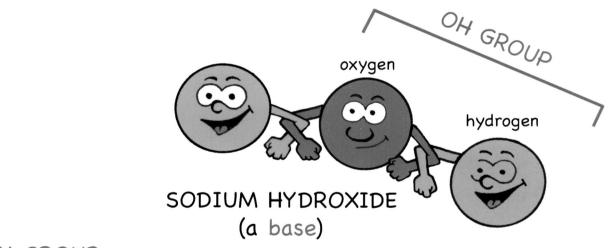

SODIUM HYDROXIDE
(a base)

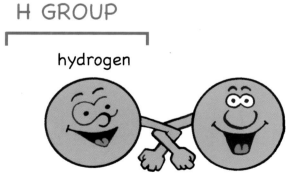

HYDROGEN CHLORIDE
(an acid)

## 3.4 Both Are Important

Both acids and bases are very important. They are needed in lots of very useful chemical reactions. You have a strong acid inside your stomach to break down your food. Without the acid in our stomachs, we could not digest our food.

Acids are also found in batteries, lemons, oranges, grapes, and even soda pop.

These things have acids in them.

Bases are found in lots of cleaners, like window cleaner, bathroom cleaner, and soap. They are also found in some foods like bananas and dates. Bases are even used to make your stomach feel better! We'll see why in the next chapter.

These things
have bases
in them.

# 3.5 Observing Acids and Bases

Chemists can use basic tools to see an acid-base reaction. Some acids and bases give off heat or explode when they react. Other times we cannot tell when an acid-base reaction happens. When we can't see an acid-base reaction, we can put something into the acid-base mixture that will show us that the reaction is taking place. This "something" is called an indicator because it indicates, or tells us, something is happening or has happened.

# Indicators

We use different kinds of indicators all the time. Stop lights indicate when we can go or when we should stop. When we turn on the oven, an indicator tells us when it is hot enough. A thermometer is an indicator. It can tell when your body has a fever. Indicators are also used in chemistry.

An acid-base indicator tells us whether we have an acid or a base. There are different kinds of acid-base indicators. A simple acid-base indicator is red cabbage juice! Red cabbage juice turns pink with acids and green with bases.

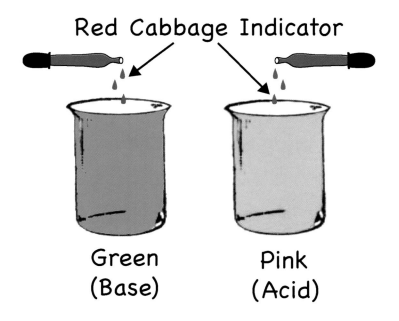

Red Cabbage Indicator

Green
(Base)

Pink
(Acid)

# 3.6 Summary

○  Acids taste sour.

○  Bases taste bitter and are slippery.

○  Acids have an H group, and bases have an OH group.

○  Acids and bases are found everywhere—in batteries, in your stomach, in household cleaners, and even in bananas and lemons!

○  An acid-base indicator tells us whether we have an acid or a base.

# Chapter 4    Acids and Bases React

## 4.1 When Acids and Bases Meet

In the last chapter we learned about two different kinds of molecules—acids and bases. We saw that acids and bases are found in lots of different things. Acids are in batteries, lemons, and even soda pop. Bases are in soap, window cleaner, and bananas too.

What happens when acids and bases meet? When molecules meet, sometimes they react. Do acids and bases react when they meet?

**1.** ## An acid and a base meet.

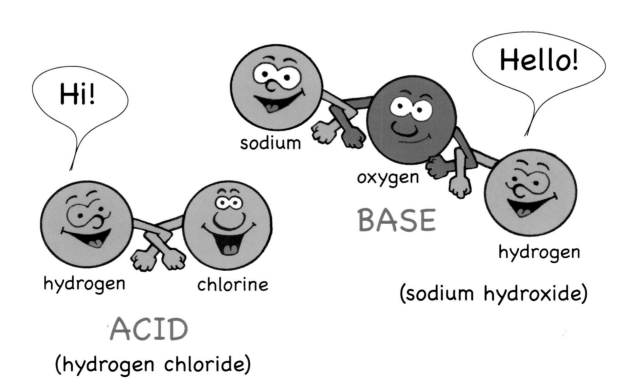

Hi!

sodium

Hello!

oxygen

BASE

hydrogen    chlorine

hydrogen

(sodium hydroxide)

ACID

(hydrogen chloride)

# 4.2 Acid-Base Reactions

In fact, they do! Acids and bases make a special kind of reaction called an acid-base reaction. When an acid and a base meet, the atoms in the acid exchange with the atoms in the base.

After they meet, some atoms leave their molecules.

**2.** The atoms leave their molecules.

Next, the atoms that left their molecules go to the other molecules and "make new friends."

**3.** The atoms make new friends.

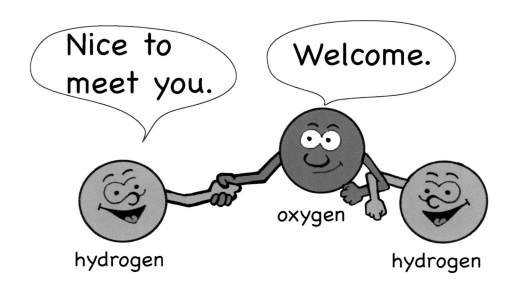

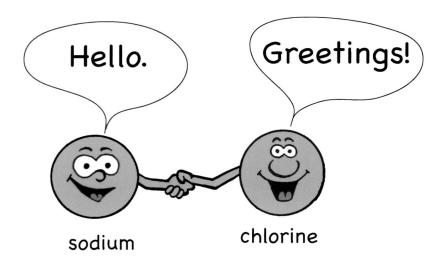

Now two new molecules have been made. The new molecules for this reaction are water and table salt (sodium chloride).

## 4. Two new molecules are made.

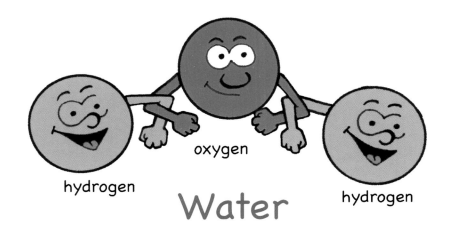

Water

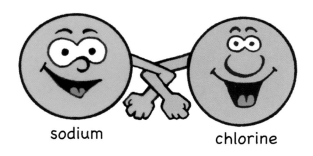

## Table Salt
## (sodium chloride)

The acids and bases are no longer acids and bases. When they react, they become other kinds of molecules, such as salt and water.

# 4.3 Important Acid-Base Reactions

Acid-base reactions are very important. For example, your stomach has acid in it. This acid is necessary for digesting your food. Sometimes there is too much acid. When this happens, your stomach hurts. The medicine your mom or

dad may give you is a base. It reacts with the acid in your stomach, turning it into a salt and water. That makes your stomach stop hurting.

# 4.4 Summary

- Acids and bases react with each other in acid-base reactions.

- When an acid and a base meet in an acid-base reaction, atoms in the acid exchange with atoms in the base.

- Many acid-base reactions make salts and water.

- Acid-base reactions are very important.

# Chapter 5   Food and Taste

Chemistry

Salty, sweet, sour! We do it all!

Don't forget bitter, too!

# 5.1 Tasty Molecules

Now you know why vinegar and lemons taste sour—they're acids! And why mineral water and soda water taste bitter—they're bases! Have you ever wondered why salt tastes salty and sugar tastes sweet?

We have learned that everything around us is made of atoms, and atoms combine to make molecules. The food we eat is made of molecules, but not all of the food we eat tastes the same. Why? Different molecules in different foods make foods taste different.

**1.** Acid molecules found in soda pop...

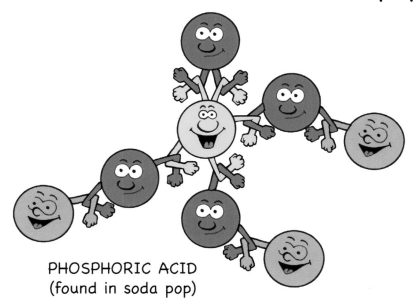

PHOSPHORIC ACID
(found in soda pop)

...make soda pop taste sour*.

(*soda pop also has lots and lots of sugar in it, so
it also tastes very sweet.)

**2.** Acid molecules in vinegar...

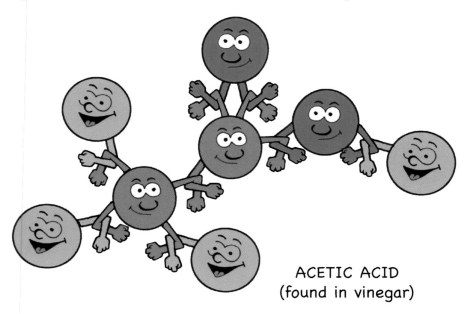

ACETIC ACID
(found in vinegar)

... make vinegar taste sour.

We have already seen that sour foods often have an acid in them. Lemons, vinegar, and grapefruit have acid in them. When you eat foods with acid in them, your tongue tells your brain "sour."

Foods that have salt in them taste salty. Salt molecules look very different from acid molecules. Remember that table salt has a sodium atom and a chlorine atom hooked together. When you eat foods with salt in them, your tongue tells your brain "salty."

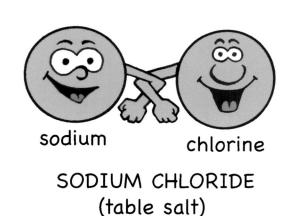

sodium          chlorine

SODIUM CHLORIDE
(table salt)

# 5.2 The Amazing Tongue

Your tongue is designed to tell your brain what kind of molecules are in your food. It can sense acids, bases, salt, sugar, and many other molecules. The tongue is essentially a tool your body uses to detect certain atoms and molecules.

For example, foods that taste sweet have sugar in them. A sugar molecule looks different from a salt molecule or an acid molecule. A sugar molecule is larger, has more atoms in it, and some of the atoms are hooked together in a ring. When you eat a piece of candy, your tongue tells your brain "sweet" because your tongue senses sugar.

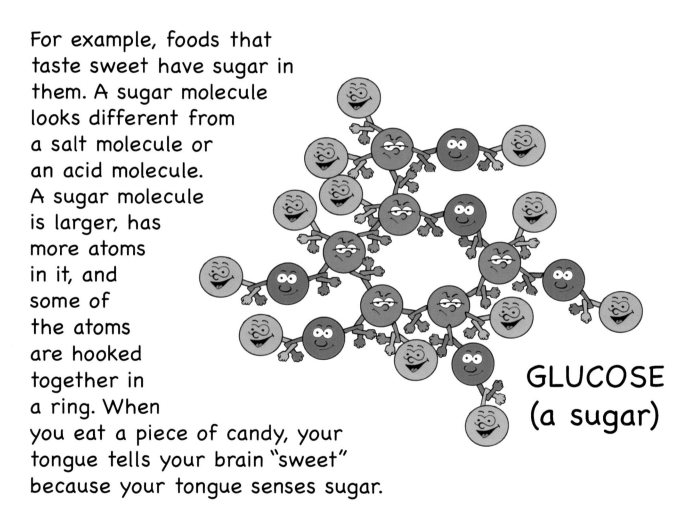

GLUCOSE
(a sugar)

Your tongue can tell the difference between a salt molecule, an acid molecule, and a sugar molecule.

Your tongue is a remarkable indicator.

Remember from Chapter 3 that an acid-base indicator tells the difference between acids and bases. There are lots of man-made indicators, like acid-base indicators, thermometers, and stop lights, but there are no indicators as intricately designed as your own tongue!

## 5.3 Large Tasty Molecules

Even though your tongue is an amazing indicator, your tongue can't taste all molecules. For example, a raw potato doesn't exactly taste sweet, salty, bitter, or sour, but something in between. In fact, a potato is made mostly of sugar molecules, but your tongue can't taste the sugar molecules in a raw potato because the molecules are hooked together in long chains called carbohydrates.

one glucose molecule

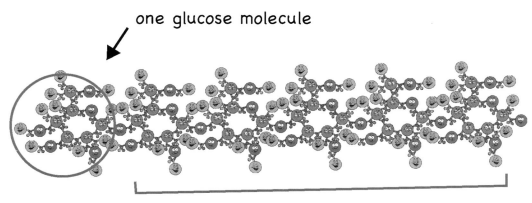

chain of glucose molecules

# CARBOHYDRATE

Many different foods have carbohydrates. Bread, pasta, potatoes, and many fruits have carbohydrates in them. Carbohydrates are important molecules for your body. Because carbohydrates are made of sugar molecules, they provide the energy your body needs to ride a bike or climb a tree!

## 5.4 Summary

○ Foods taste different because foods are made of different molecules.

○ Your tongue is an amazing indicator that can tell the difference between salts, acids, bases, and sugars.

○ Carbohydrates are long chains of sugar molecules.

○ Your tongue can't taste sugar molecules in foods that contain carbohydrates if the carbohydrates are hooked together in long chains of molecules.

# Chapter 6  Biologist's Toolbox

Biology

# 6.1 Introduction

How do you study living things? How can you look at cells or protists if they are too small to see when using only your eyes? How do you track a tiger when it can run fast and hide in the jungle? How can you measure, weigh, and monitor a hippopotamus when it is too large to fit on a balance?

Biologists use a variety of tools to measure, monitor, weigh, track, and observe living things. In this chapter we will take a look at some of the tools biologists use.

# 6.2 Brief History

People have been observing plants and animals for a very long time. Ancient people used both plants and animals for food, clothing, shelter, and as companions. Ancient civilizations learned about plants and how to create farms to grow food for large numbers of people. These civilizations also learned about animals and how to use them for food and transportation and how to tame them for pets.

Although many people observed plants and animals, historians often call Aristotle the first real biologist. Aristotle was a philosopher who lived in Greece from 384-322 B.C.E.

**ARISTOTLE** 384-322 BCE

Aristotle was the first person to organize plants and animals into categories. He was particularly interested in studying the *differences* between various plants and animals. He believed that the first step to understanding plants and animals was to look at all the ways in which they were different. He observed how animals with hair are different from animals without hair and how animals with paws are different from animals with hooves. His most valuable tool in studying differences was his ability to make good observations.

# 6.3 Basic Biology Tools

Today a biologist's most basic and important tool is the same as it was for Aristotle—the ability to make good observations. Biologists need to observe how plants and animals grow, live, and interact with other plants and animals. Many field biologists (those who work outdoors) take years to carefully observe and record things such as animal behavior, how different plants grow, or how changes in their surroundings affect the way plants and animals live.

Another basic tool used by biologists is the field notebook. A field notebook is essential for recording observations. Field notebooks can be large or small, print or digital. In the field notebook a biologist records the date, time of day, location, and the plants or animals being observed. Some biologists draw pictures directly in their field notebook, and many biologists carry a camera or video recorder to capture their observations.

A magnifying glass is a basic tool that can be very helpful for a biologist. A magnifying glass makes small things appear larger. For example, if you leave your pie outside, you might discover in the morning that ants have come to have a taste. You can see the ants with your eyes, but if you use a magnifying glass, you can see them even more clearly. They look big in the magnifying glass, and you can see the hair on their legs, the smoothness of their backs, and the number of pie crumbs they are taking.

# 6.4 Advanced Biology Tools

Biology covers a broad range of specialized subjects. For this reason there are many different kinds of advanced tools that biologists use.

Some biologists study plants and might use kits to test soils or water quality. Other

biologists study animals and might use sophisticated tracking equipment, cameras, and airplanes. Some biologists who study animals that live in the oceans will use boats, shark cages, or submarines.

Many biologists use microscopes to see very small objects and tiny creatures. A microscope is a special kind of tool that helps you look at things too small for your eyes alone to see.

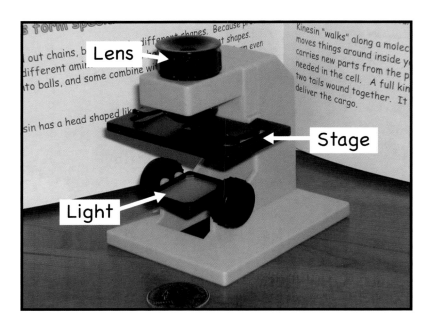

A microscope is like a magnifying glass in that it makes very small things look big. A microscope has a lens, usually made of glass. The lens magnifies (makes whatever you are seeing look bigger) like a magnifying glass does. But a microscope is also different from a magnifying glass. For example, a microscope has a stage where you put the sample (the thing you want to see—like pond water or ocean water). The stage helps keep the sample still while it is being observed.

Also, a microscope usually has a little light that makes the sample brighter and easier to see. In some microscopes, the light comes from a little mirror that captures room light and reflects it back through the microscope. Other microscopes use a tiny light bulb under the stage to illuminate the sample being observed.

# 6.5 Summary

● Biologists use a variety of basic and advanced tools to do experiments and make good observations.

● Aristotle was the first biologist who tried to organize plants and animals into groups.

● The most important tool for a biologist is the ability to make good observations.

● Biologists use lots of different tools to study plants and animals, such as microscopes, boats, tracking equipment, and cameras.

# Chapter 7  Protists Move

Biology

# 7.1 Tiny Creatures

How tiny is the smallest living creature? If you look at yourself, you might think you are pretty small compared to your dad, but are you the smallest living creature? No! You are not as small as your cat. The cat is smaller than you are. But is a cat the smallest living thing? No. In fact, the cat chases (and sometimes eats) moths or birds or mice that are smaller than the cat.

How about a moth? Do you think the moth is the smallest living creature?

No. A ladybug is smaller than a moth, and an ant is smaller than a ladybug, and a gnat is even smaller than an ant. So how small is the smallest living creature?

The smallest living creatures are so small that you can't even see them when looking with just your eyes. There is a whole world of tiny creatures that you can't see that live in ponds, in oceans, in dirt, and even inside of you!

One type of tiny creature you can't see with only your eyes is called a protist (also called a protozoan). A protist is a small creature that can do many of the things bigger creatures (like you) can do. Protists can crawl and swim and eat and sense light. Protists are very small but can do amazing things.

To observe protozoa (protists), you have to use a microscope. The first person to see protists was a man from Holland named Anton van Leeuwenhoek. With his microscope he saw little animals in pond water. He also found them in his mouth!

# 7.2 Different Kinds of Tiny Creatures

There are many different kinds of protists that can be seen only with a microscope. But how do you know what kinds of creatures you are seeing?

When scientists sort living things into groups, they are easier to study. The kingdom Protista is a very large group with over sixty thousand different kinds of protists. Because it is such a large group, scientists need to sort the protists into even smaller groups.

# 7.3 Sorting Protists

One way to sort protists into smaller groups is to notice the different ways protists move and then group them by how they move.

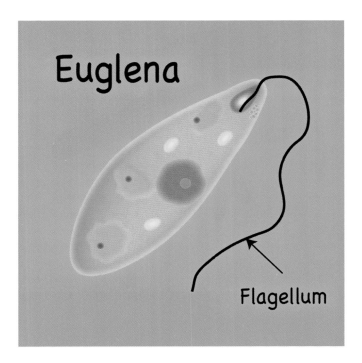

Euglena

Flagellum

One way protists move is to swim with a long tail called a flagellum. Some protists, like euglena, have a flagellum. Protists that move by using a flagellum are called Flagellates.

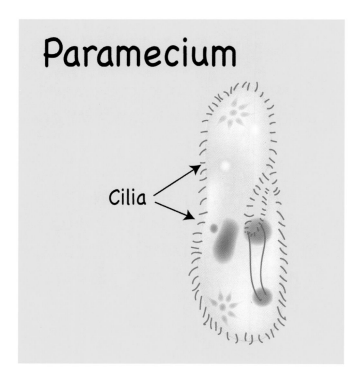

## Paramecium

Cilia

Another way protists move is by using small hairlike features called cilia. Cilia beat fast in the water, making the protists move forwards and backwards and sideways. A paramecium uses cilia to move. Protozoa that move with cilia are called Ciliates.

Some protists move by crawling. Amoebas are protists that use false feet called pseudopods to crawl from one place to another. Protists that use false feet to move are called Amoeboids.

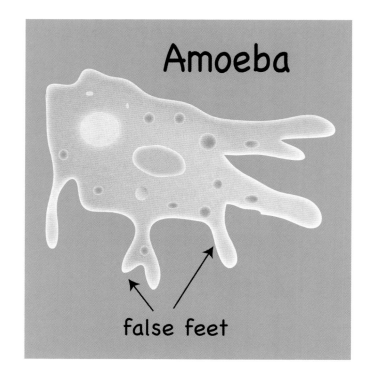

## Amoeba

false feet

# 7.4 Summary

- There are many small creatures that we cannot see by using just our eyes.

- Scientists use a microscope to see small creatures.

- Protists (also called protozoa) are small creatures that can be found in pond water and ocean water.

- One way scientists sort protists is by how they move. Three groups of protists are Flagellates, Ciliates, and Amoeboids.

- Many protists move by using a flagellum, by using cilia, or by using pseudopods (false feet) to crawl.

# Chapter 8  Protists Eat

Biology

# 8.1 Euglena Eat

A euglena uses sunlight to make its own food. It changes sunlight to food by using chloroplasts. Chloroplasts are special parts inside a cell. A chloroplast contains chlorophyll which is a green substance that captures sunlight. Because chlorophyll is green, it gives euglena their green color.

A euglena will swim toward the sunlight that it uses to make food. A euglena has a little eyespot that helps it know where to find the sunlight.

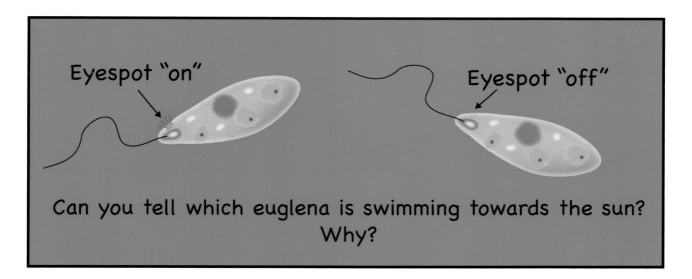

Eyespot "on"

Eyespot "off"

Can you tell which euglena is swimming towards the sun?
Why?

# 8.2 Paramecia Eat

Not all protists can make their own food like a euglena does. A paramecium has to go find its food, just like we do! But a paramecium cannot go to the grocery store for eggs and milk like we can. It must swim around with its cilia to look for food in the water.

A paramecium eats other small creatures, such as other protozoa or bacteria. The paramecium has a mouth that it uses to capture food. The mouth does not move like a human mouth and it doesn't have any teeth.

The cilia around the mouth move, or beat, rapidly. This makes the water near the mouth of the paramecium swirl. Take your hands and move them in some water, and you can feel the water swirling around your hands.

A paramecium uses the swirling water to move food toward its mouth. When the food enters the mouth of the paramecium, it travels through a small tube into a tiny stomach and gets digested. The paramecium takes what it needs from the digested food, and the unused food is pushed out through a small hole.

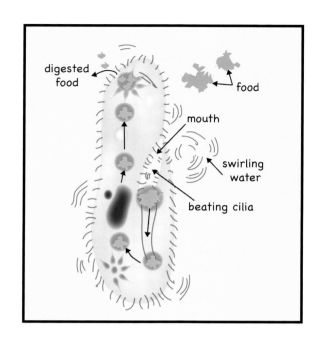

Although a paramecium has only one cell, it can move, eat, and digest food just like larger creatures. For being so small, the paramecium is an amazing creature.

## 8.3 Amoebas Eat

An amoeba eats with its feet! Can you imagine eating with your feet? It would be pretty hard for you to eat with your feet, but it isn't hard at all for an amoeba.

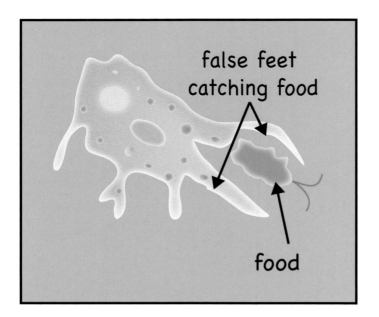

false feet catching food

food

An amoeba uses its false feet, or pseudopods, to surround the food it wants to eat. Once the food is surrounded, the amoeba brings its feet together and makes something like a stomach out of the false feet that surround the food.

The stomach then absorbs the food into the body of the amoeba. That is how the amoeba eats with its feet!

# 8.4 Other Protists Eat

There are other protists that eat in other ways. For example, a protist called a *Coleps* rotates its whole body to swim through the water.

It also rotates as it eats. As it rotates, it uses its sharp teeth to bore through the food like a tiny drill. Then it eats the food it removes from the hole it has made with its teeth.

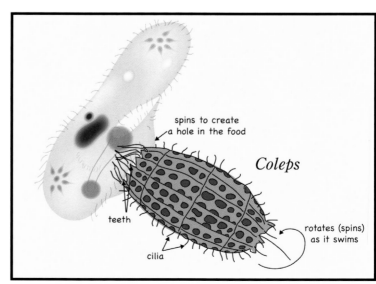

spins to create a hole in the food

*Coleps*

teeth

rotates (spins) as it swims

cilia

# 8.5 Summary

- A euglena uses chloroplasts to make its food.

- A paramecium uses cilia to swirl the water and sweep food into its mouth.

- An ameoba uses its pseudopods, or false feet, to capture food and eat.

- Other protists use other ways to eat.

# Chapter 9  Fungi: Molds, Mushrooms, Yeasts

Biology

# 9.1 Introduction

Have you ever eaten a mushroom? Some people love mushrooms, and other people don't like them at all.

Because mushrooms remind us of plants, we often think of mushrooms as being plants. Mushrooms grow in the ground, like plants, and can be found in the forest, like plants, but a mushroom is not a plant. A mushroom is a fungus. Mushrooms are different from plants because plants make their own food while mushrooms get their food by eating dead plants and animals.

Fungi (plural of fungus) have a whole kingdom, just like plants and animals do. There are three kinds of fungi—molds, mushrooms, and yeast. All fungi are similar in some ways, and they all break down materials to get their food.

# 9.2 Molds

Molds are small fungi and are found everywhere. They can be in the soil, on wood, on dead plants, and on our food. Molds come in many different colors. They can be brown, white, orange, green, or black. Some molds are safe to eat, such as the mold in bleu cheese, but many molds will make us sick. People can be allergic to molds that are around them, and some molds on food can cause illnesses.

Molds need water and food to grow, and they like to grow in warm places. Molds reproduce by making spores. Spores are too tiny to see and are usually made of just one cell. Given the right conditions, each spore can grow into a new mold. When we clean up the kitchen, we are cleaning up mold spores that we can't see. Cleaning up water and food stops molds from growing by removing their source of nutrients. We throw out bad food if it has mold on it because eating it could make us sick.

# 9.3 Mushrooms

Mushrooms grow in a variety of different shapes, sizes, and colors. Many mushrooms have a stem and a cap and look like tiny umbrellas.

Other mushrooms are shaped like cups and may or may not have a stem.

Mushrooms break down food and grow from their hyphae. Hyphae are very thin threads that spread out in the soil and are used by the mushroom to gather nutrients from the soil. In this way hyphae are similar to the roots of a plant. Hyphae are used by a mushroom to break down dead or decaying

leaves, wood, or animals to use for food. By breaking down dead things, mushrooms help clean up and remove the dead things.

Like molds, mushrooms reproduce by making spores and most mushroom spores are also too tiny to see.

Mushroom hunters are careful to gather only the kinds of mushrooms they know about because some mushrooms are very poisonous. You should not eat a mushroom that you have found outside of a grocery store unless a mushroom expert can tell you it is safe to eat.

## 9.4 Yeasts

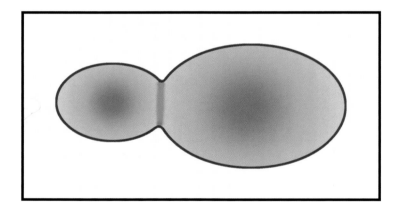

Yeasts are fungi that we use in making bread, desserts, beer, and wine. Yeasts are some of the smallest fungi and are made of only one cell. A yeast reproduces by dividing its cell in two. This is called budding. Each of the two cells then grows until it is full size and can divide again.

Yeasts like to eat sugar. Like other fungi, yeasts like to be warm and moist and have lots of food. When you put yeast and sugar into warm water, the yeast will eat the sugar.

As the yeast eats sugar, it creates carbon dioxide gas as a waste product. Yeast does this even when it has bread dough all around it! The carbon dioxide gas made by the yeast makes the bubbles you see in bread. The yeast dies when bread is baked. Oven temperatures are too hot for yeast.

## 9.5 Summary

- Some fungi help us, but other fungi ruin food and can make us sick.

- Mushrooms grow from hyphae which are root-like structures in the soil.

- Molds and mushrooms reproduce by making spores.

- Yeasts reproduce by budding—dividing one cell in half to make two cells.

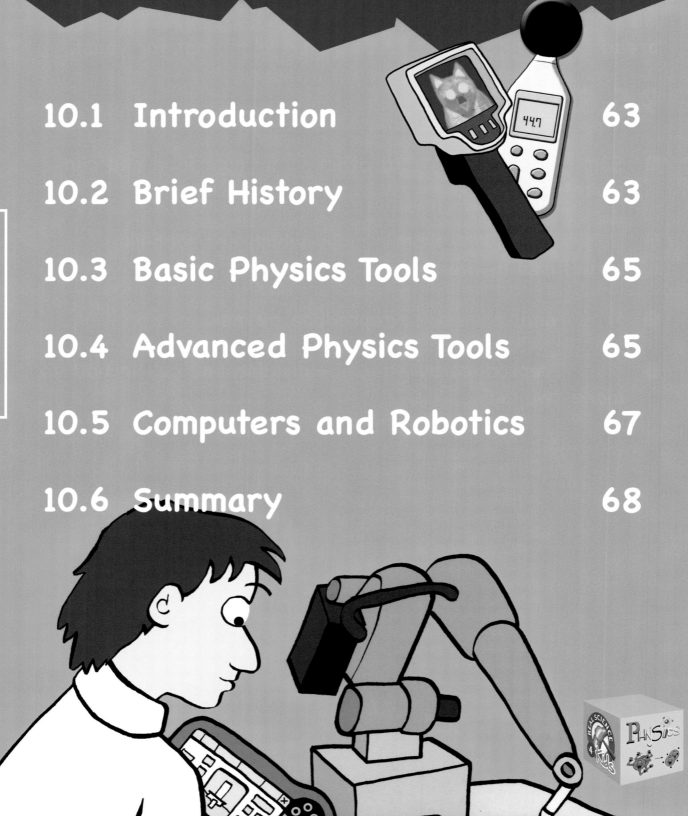

# Chapter 10  Physicist's Toolbox

Physics

# 10.1 Introduction

How do you study what happens when you throw a ball in the air? How do you find out why a marble rolls? How do you measure heat and what is happening when you rub your hands together and they get warm?

Physicists study things like motion, heat, energy, and power. Since these things are sometimes hard to see and understand, physicists use tools that help them measure, map, and record how the world around them works.

# 10.2 Brief History

Physics is considered by some scholars to be the oldest and most basic science. Ancient philosophers thought a great deal about how the world works. One of these early philosophers was Thales of Miletus (625-545 B.C.E.). Thales was born in Greece, and he traveled to Egypt where he learned about geometry and astronomy.

**THALES** 625-545 BCE

**IBN AL HAYTHAM**
965–1040 CE

Greece was not the only place where philosophers were trying to understand how the world works. Ancient scholars in the Middle East, India, and China were all thinking about how the world works. The Muslim philosopher Ibn al-Haytham studied light and how light rays travel.

Omar Khayyam was a Persian scientist who accurately calculated the length of a year.

**OMAR KHAYYAM**
1048–1131 CE

**SHEN KUO**
1031–1095 CE

In China Shen Kuo was the first to describe the magnetic needle compass.

# 10.3 Basic Physics Tools

Physicists study the world by measuring, mapping, and monitoring how things work. Physicists want to know things like how far away something is or how long it takes something to go from point A to point B. Physicists need to know details, and to find those details physicists measure distances, times, weights, and temperatures. Some

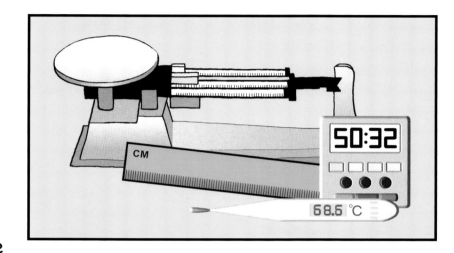

of the basic tools physicists use are timers, rulers, balances, and thermometers.

# 10.4 Advanced Physics

Physics covers a broad range of specialized subjects. Because there are so many subjects, there are many different kinds of tools.

Physicists who study sound might use a sound meter to measure high and low sounds.

Physicists who study the properties of objects and materials might use different dynamic testing machines to find out more about what these things are like.

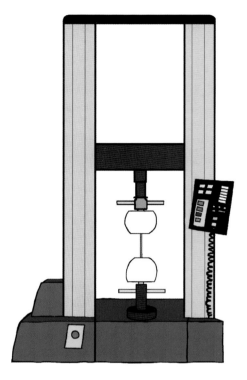

Some physicists study how objects go from hot to cold and might use a thermal imager to observe small changes in temperature.

Physicists who study electricity might use an oscilloscope to measure electrical waves.

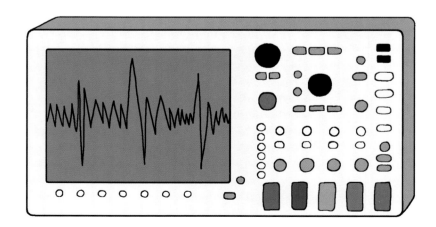

# 10.5 Computers and Robotics

Most advanced tools have computers inside or connect to a computer. In physics, computers are a very valuable tool. Computers can be programmed to collect large amounts of data. Computers can also be programmed to do complicated calculations or keep track of small distances.

Some high-level physics experiments use robots to move delicate instruments or record important information. Both computers and robotics have helped physicists learn more about how the world works.

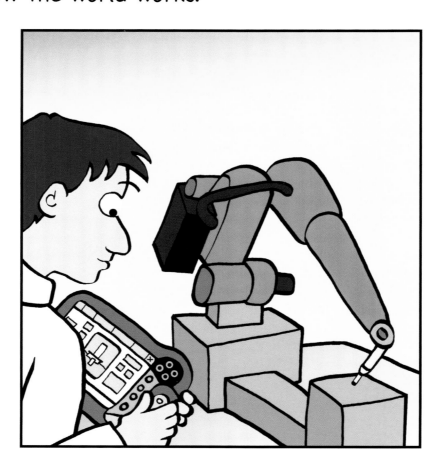

# 10.6 Summary

- Physicists use a variety of basic tools and advanced tools (instruments) to do experiments.

- Many early philosophers from Greece, the Middle East, India, and China thought about how things work.

- Physicists use basic tools like rulers, timers, balances, and thermometers.

- Physicists use advanced tools (instruments) to measure movement, temperatures, sound, and electricity.

- Computers and robots help physicists make different kinds of measurements, collect large amounts of data, and do complicated calculations, among many other tasks.

# Chapter 11 When Things Move

Physics

# 11.1 Moving Objects

A force is any action that changes the location or shape of an object or how fast or slowly an object is moving. You might think that forces also keep objects moving. This is what Aristotle thought. Aristotle was a philosopher in ancient Greece who studied how objects move. Aristotle thought that objects move because forces push on them from behind. However, 2,000 years later Galileo, an Italian physicist and astronomer, discovered that forces don't keep objects moving. Forces actually stop objects from moving. Forces can also change the direction of a moving object. But forces don't keep objects moving.

# 11.2 Keeping Objects in Motion

Galileo discovered that once an object is moving, it will keep moving unless it is stopped by a force. Forces can start an object moving or stop it, but forces do not keep an object moving. So, what keeps an object moving? An object keeps moving because of inertia. But what is inertia?

Have you ever been playing with your friends on the back porch when your mom called you to dinner? Maybe you didn't want to go to dinner. Maybe you wanted to keep playing. Maybe you even refused to stop playing and didn't go to dinner. That is inertia.

Inertia is when an object resists a change in motion. When you kept playing with your friend and did not want to change what you were doing to go to dinner, you had inertia. You didn't want to change your motion (playing) to a new motion (going to dinner). When you resisted going to dinner, you were like an object that doesn't want to stop moving. That is inertia.

Inertia also keeps objects still. When an object is moving, it wants to stay moving, and when an object is still, it wants to stay still. When an object does not want to change from moving to still or from still to moving, we say it has inertia.

# 11.3 Marbles and Bowling Balls

Everything has inertia. Bananas, oranges, bowling balls and marbles all have inertia. You have inertia. If you are standing in the middle of your room refusing to put your pajamas on, that is inertia. If you are running down a hill and you can't stop, that is inertia. So whether you are moving or not moving, you have inertia. Whether you are tall or short, young or old, you have inertia. Everything that has mass has inertia. But what is mass?

In physics, inertia comes from a property called mass. Everything has inertia because everything has mass. Simply put, mass is how heavy something is. A heavy bowling ball has more inertia than a light marble. Because a bowling ball weighs more (has more mass) than a marble, it has more inertia.

Think about how hard it is to roll a bowling ball. Now think about how easy it is to roll a marble. It is harder to get

a bowling ball to move than it is to get a marble to move. Why? Because a bowling ball has more inertia. It is also harder to get a bowling ball to stop moving than it is to stop a marble. Why? Again, because a bowling ball has more inertia than a marble.

# 11.4 Friction

We said that objects don't stop moving unless a force makes them stop. Because everything has inertia, an object in motion will stay in motion.

But wait! If you roll a soccer ball on the soccer field, it will eventually stop even if another soccer player doesn't make it stop. Why? Why does a soccer ball stop moving even if no one is there to make it stop?

It stops moving because of friction. Remember, all objects will keep moving (because all objects have inertia) unless a force makes them stop moving. Everywhere on Earth, friction makes things stop moving. Friction is a force that stops objects from moving.

Friction can come from almost anything. The grass in the soccer field makes friction that stops the rolling soccer ball. If a ball is thrown into a swimming pool, the ball will eventually stop moving because of the friction created by the water. Even air creates friction. If a ball is thrown into the sky, it will eventually slow down and stop moving because of friction caused by the air.

# 11.5 Summary

- A force is any action that changes the location or shape of an object or how fast or slowly an object is moving.

- Forces make objects start to move, and forces also stop objects from moving. But forces do not keep objects moving.

- Inertia keeps objects still and keeps objects moving.

- Simply put, mass is how heavy something is.

- Friction is a force that will stop objects that are moving.

# Chapter 12  Linear Motion

Physics

# 12.1 Introduction

In the last chapter we explored kinetic energy, or moving energy. In this chapter we are going to look at a specific kind of motion called linear motion. Linear motion is simply motion that occurs along a line. If you push a hockey puck straight in front of you, it has linear motion. If you throw a baseball straight into the catcher's mitt, it has linear motion.

# 12.2 How Far?

Did you know that everything is moving? Even objects you think are standing still are moving. Your house is moving and even mountains are moving! You can tell houses and mountains are moving because you can see the Sun shine on them in the morning and then stop shining on them at night. Your house and the mountains around you are moving because the Earth is moving as it spins around and around on its axis. The Earth is also moving around the Sun.

Physicists say that motion is relative. This means that we measure the motion of an object by comparing it to other objects. Physicists use the term speed to mean how fast an object moves. The speed of an object is *relative* to the objects surrounding it. For example, if a police officer pulls you over and hands you a speeding ticket, it is because you were moving too fast compared to him, the road, and the houses around him.

The speed of an object is the measure of how far it goes in a given time. If you start at your back porch and run to the back wall of your yard and it takes you three minutes, you ran that distance at a certain speed. But if your friend runs to the back wall of your yard and finishes the same distance in only one minute, then your friend ran faster than you did. A physicist would say your friend ran with more speed.

# 12.3 Average Speed

Physicists like to study details. If you ran to the back wall three times, a physicist would observe your speed the first time, the second time, and the third time you ran. The physicist would clock how fast you ran each time and would record three

separate times. The speed at which you ran might have been affected by different things. For instance, if you got more tired each time you ran, your speed might have been slower the second time you ran and even slower the third time.

Imagine that you want to know on average how fast you can run to the back wall of your yard. To find your average speed you would add all three of your times together and then divide by three. This would tell you on average how fast you ran.

Knowing your average speed is useful information. You might find out that on average you can run to the back wall in two minutes, but on days when you feel really good you can run this distance on average in less than two minutes. By recording your average speed each day and making notes about how you were feeling and other things such as what you had for breakfast, you can compare your good days and your bad days and learn about what helps you run faster.

# 12.4 Acceleration

Imagine that you are running to the back wall and suddenly your friend starts to run beside you. You might try to win the race, so you speed up! Then as you get near the end, you might start to get tired and have to slow down.

When you started to run faster, you changed your acceleration. In physics, acceleration is the change in speed of a moving object for a given time. For example, if you roll a marble down a ramp, you can watch it accelerate as it gets closer to the ground. The marble will start slowly and then gradually speed up. Depending on how long your ramp is, the marble might be moving very fast when it hits the ground. Because the marble speeds up as it travels down the ramp, physicists say it accelerates—changes its speed as it moves.

## 12.5 Summary

- Linear motion is the motion of an object in a straight line.

- Speed is how fast an object travels.

- Average speed is calculated by measuring the speed of an object several times, adding the speeds together, and dividing the total by the number of times the speed was measured.

- An object accelerates when it changes its speed while it is moving.

# Chapter 13  Non-Linear Motion

**Physics**

A

B

# 13.1 Introduction

In the last chapter we saw how the speed of an object can be measured when it is moving in a straight line. We learned that movement in a straight line is called linear motion. In this chapter we are going to look at non-linear motion, or what happens when an object is not moving in a straight line.

# 13.2 Throwing a Ball

What happens if you go outside and throw a ball across your backyard? The ball moves forward, relative to your position, and travels to the other side of the yard. In the last chapter, we discovered that this type of motion is called *linear motion.*

But the ball not only moves forward, it also moves up and down. The up and down motion forms a curved path. Because this path is curved and not straight, it is called non-linear motion. Non-linear motion is motion that does not follow a straight line.

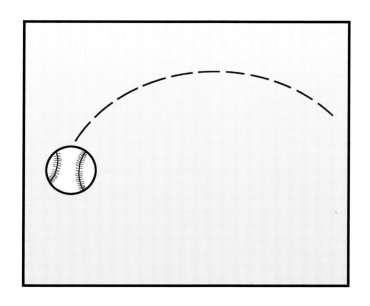

# 13.3 Riding a Bike

When you sit on a bike and push the pedals, you are using your legs to move you and your bike forward. If you are pedaling your bike and you look down at the frame of the bike, you will see that both you and the bike frame are moving forward in a straight line. This is an example of linear motion.

However, if you look below the bike frame and notice the wheels, you will see that the wheels are turning as you pedal. In physics, we call this type of motion non-linear motion. The wheels are traveling in a circle, around the center hub. We could say the wheels are rotating. Also, because the wheels are traveling in an exact circle, they are moving with a special type of non-linear motion called rotational motion.

One way to observe the rotational motion of a bike wheel is to put a blue dot on the rear wheel and prop the bike up so the rear wheel is off the ground. As the pedals are pushed, the rear wheel moves, and the blue dot travels in a circle. This makes it easy to see the rotational motion of the wheel.

Bicycle wheels, car wheels, motorcycle wheels, airplane propellers, and even CDs move with rotational motion. In the case of bicycles, cars, motorcycles, and airplanes, the rotational motion of the wheels and propellers is converted to linear motion as the vehicle moves forward. In the case of a CD spinning in a CD player or in a computer, the movement of the CD is not converted to linear motion but to sound. However, in all cases, the wheels, propellers, and CDs are moving with rotational motion. They are all moving in a circle.

## 13.4 Easy and Hard Gears

Have you ever used a bike to go fast on a flat street? And have you ever used a bike to climb slowly up a steep hill? If you have a bike with more than one gear, you probably used a hard gear to go fast on a flat street and an easy gear to climb up a hill.

On a bicycle, gears are simple machines that use rotational motion to make it easier to climb hills and go fast on flat streets.

If you look carefully at the pedals of a single gear bicycle, you will see that they are attached to a metal wheel that has teeth. If you look at the rear wheel, you will see another metal wheel with teeth. Each of these metal wheels with teeth is called a sprocket. A chain goes around both of the two sprockets, joining them together.

When you use the pedals to turn the front sprocket, the chain transfers this motion to the sprocket on the back wheel, turning the wheel and moving the bicycle forward.

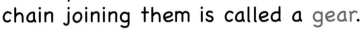

The combination of front sprocket, back sprocket, and the chain joining them is called a gear.

If you look at a bike that has more than one gear, you will see that it has several different size sprockets on the front and several different size sprockets on the back. By combining different sizes of front and back sprockets, you can make the bike easier or harder to pedal.

If the front sprocket is much larger than the back sprocket, the gear is harder to pedal but makes the back wheel move very fast. On a flat surface this gear is used for speed.

If the front sprocket is smaller than the back sprocket, the gear is easier to pedal but moves the back wheel very slowly. Because the gear is easier to pedal, this gear can be used to climb hills.

By understanding how gears work, you can pick gears to help you go uphill with less effort and downhill faster!

# 13.5 Summary

- Non-linear motion is motion of an object that moves in a curve or in a circle.

- Rotational motion is a type of non-linear motion of an object that rotates or moves in a circle.

- Bicycles, cars, motorcycles, and airplane propellers use rotational motion of the wheel or propeller to move them forward.

- The gears on a bicycle use rotational motion. Different size sprockets are used to make a bike go faster or make it easier to climb hills.

# Chapter 14   Geologist's Toolbox

Geology

# 14.1 Introduction

Geologists are scientists who use special tools to study Earth. Some tools are basic, like hammers and lenses, and some tools are more advanced, like seismographs and submarines.

There are different tools for different types of geologists. Some geologists study what things are made of and may use test tubes and chemicals to test minerals and rocks. Some geologists study how things are put together and might use hammers and microscopes to examine layers of sediments and inside rocks.

Because there are many different types of geologists, there are many different types of tools in a geologist's toolbox.

# 14.2 Brief History

It's difficult to know exactly what the first geology tool was and when it was invented. It is clear from a variety of ancient texts that early geologists were curious about what was inside rocks and beneath layers of dirt, and they likely used simple tools such as hammers and shovels to examine rocks and minerals.

Theophrastus was a student of Aristotle and wrote a book called *On Stones* in which he describes the color, hardness, and smoothness of a variety of both common and rare stones. Many of these stones were found on the ground, in streams, and by mining.

**THEOPHRASTUS**
372-287 BCE

It is also clear from writings of Theophrastus that he explored the nature of stones by performing various experiments. By using fire, he could observe which stones melted or changed color when burned. Theophrastus also used acids to examine which stones would dissolve and which would withstand these chemical tests.

## 14.3 Basic Tools: Hammers and Lenses

Three types of rock hammers used by geologists are: the pointed tip rock hammer, the chisel edge rock hammer, and the crack hammer.

A pointed tip rock hammer has one end that comes to a point. The other end has a head that is flat and square. Pointed tip rock hammers are also called rock picks, and they are generally used by geologists when they are working with hard rocks. Geologists often use the pointy tip to dig fossil samples out of rocks and the square end to crack open a rock to see what's inside.

A chisel edge rock hammer has one end that is flat and broad like a chisel rather than being pointy. The other end is a square head. The chisel end is used to split layers of soft rock. The square head is used to crack open rocks.

A crack hammer has two blunt ends. It is usually heavier than either a pointed tip rock hammer or a chisel edge rock hammer. Its heaviness can make it easier for geologists to break rocks open.

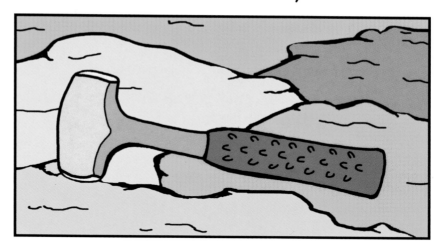

Once a geologist breaks a rock open with a rock hammer, is there a way to get a better look at what's inside? To

better see the features of the inside of a rock, geologists often use a hand lens. A hand lens is a small magnifier that folds into a holder, making it compact and easy to carry. A hand lens can be carried in a pocket or on a string around the neck.

A hand lens magnifies a rock, making it easier to see. With a hand lens, a geologist can look at the details of a rock. This can help determine what the rock is made of.

# 14.4 Advanced Geology Tools

Modern geologists use a variety of advanced tools to study Earth's rocks, minerals, soils, and Earth's activity. Computers, satellites, radios, and other modern technologies play a very important role in how geologists collect and analyze data.

A global positioning system or GPS is an electronic device that has greatly changed how geologists map and study Earth's surface. A GPS device receives signals from a network of satellites orbiting the Earth. The GPS unit then uses this data to calculate its location on the Earth. Many GPS devices are small enough to be easily tucked into a backpack or pocket. Geologists use GPS devices to help them do things such as navigate, create geographical maps, locate specific landmarks, and determine property lines.

Another advanced technology that has helped geologists map Earth's surface is the geographic information system or GIS. A GIS is a system that uses computers to gather and sort different types of geographical data. The data can then be used to create maps that help geologist examine mountains, rivers, volcanoes, earthquakes, and even geological features beneath the ocean!

## 14.5 Summary

- ○ Geologists use both basic and advanced tools.

- ○ Many geologists use basic tools such as rock hammers and hand lenses.

- ○ Geologists also use advanced electronic tools such as the GPS (global positioning system).

- ○ Computers play an important role in the study of geology. Geologists use computer systems, such as GIS (geographic information system), to study Earth's crust.

# Chapter 15  Earth's Spheres

Geology

# 15.1 Introduction

If you go outside and walk around in your backyard, you will notice a variety of features that make up the place on Earth where you live.

When you jump up and down, you can feel the hard rock surface below your feet. If you have a shovel, you might dig a little way below the surface and observe dirt, rocks, and minerals. This is the "rock part" of Earth, called the crust. The crust and all of the layers of Earth below the crust together are called the geosphere.

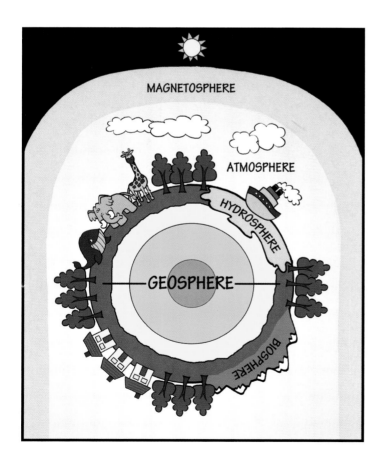

When you inhale and exhale, you feel your lungs fill with oxygen and then release carbon dioxide. This is the "air part" of Earth called the atmosphere.

If you walk on the grass or kneel down to examine tiny ants taking off with crumbs from your peanut butter sandwich, you are looking at the "biology part" of Earth called the biosphere.

If it starts to rain on you while you are looking at the ants scurrying on the ground and carrying your sandwich crumbs, you are experiencing the "water part" of Earth called the hydrosphere.

And finally, if you use a compass to find your way home, you are interacting with the "magnetic part" of Earth called the magnetic field which is within the magnetosphere. The magnetosphere is the area surrounding Earth in space where Earth's magnetic field interacts with gases given off by the Sun.

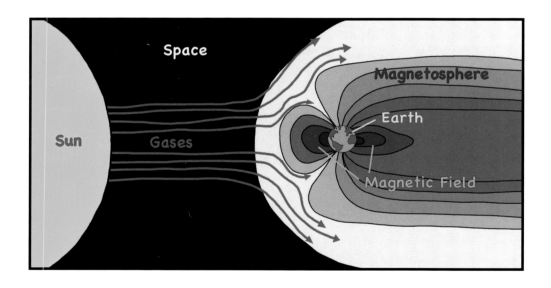

The geosphere, atmosphere, biosphere, hydrosphere, and magnetosphere can be studied both separately and together. As a whole, they make up this planet we know as Earth.

## 15.2 Why Spheres?

Notice that all of these names end in the term sphere. The word sphere refers to a ball-shaped object. The Earth is a ball-shaped or *spherical* object in space.

When geologists talk about any of the "spheres" of Earth, they are talking about a whole part, or layer, that encircles the Earth. The geosphere refers to all of the rock and mineral layers that make up Earth's surface and interior. The atmosphere is the whole layer of air that covers Earth. The biosphere contains all the living things that inhabit Earth. The hydrosphere has all the water that is found on Earth, and the magnetosphere includes the entire magnetic field of Earth.

When geologists study a particular part of a layer of the Earth, they use words that describe specific features. For example, mountains, rocks, and the ocean floor are different parts of the geosphere. Oceans, lakes, and glaciers are different parts of the hydrosphere. A biome is a particular part of the biosphere in which the climate, soils, and plant life are similar throughout.

# 15.3 Why Study Earth's Spheres Separately?

Sometimes it helps to understand how something works by taking it apart and studying each piece separately. If you want to know more about how your bicycle works, you could take off the wheels and the tires, take off the chain, and remove the sprockets to study each part by itself.

You might discover that your bicycle frame is built out of sturdy metal and that it is hollow inside to make it lighter. You might discover that your tire tubes are made out of soft rubber and the tires are thicker with small bumps or treads that help the tires grip the road. You might also discover that the chain is flexible and can bend and that a sprocket is hard and has teeth to support and carry the chain.

By studying each piece of your bike separately, you can better understand how your bike works when it's all put together.

The same is true about studying Earth. It's useful for geologists to look carefully at each sphere and learn everything they can about water or air or the rocks that make up Earth. Also, because there is so much to learn, no one person can study everything. This is one reason geologists specialize in different areas of geology. A geochemist may focus only on studying the water in the oceans, and a structural geologist may only study the mountains beneath the oceans. When they work together and swap information, they both understand the oceans better.

# 15.4 Putting Them All Together

Just like your whole bike functions as a combination of different parts working together, Earth operates as a combination of different parts that work together. The atmosphere, biosphere, geosphere, hydrosphere, and magnetosphere all work together to create the planet we call Earth.

For example, when the atmosphere creates a big storm over the ocean, the hydrosphere is affected, and the biosphere and geosphere may also be affected. When animals in the biosphere, like beavers and people, build dams, it can affect the geosphere, hydrosphere, and other parts of the biosphere. When a volcano erupts, it can affect the geosphere, atmosphere, and biosphere.

By studying the individual spheres separately and then pooling all that information to study Earth as a whole, geologists can gain a more accurate picture of this world we call Earth.

# 15.5 Summary

○ Earth can be studied as a combination of different spheres.

○ The five major spheres that make up Earth are the geosphere, atmosphere, biosphere, hydrosphere, and magnetosphere.

○ Studying each sphere separately helps scientists learn more about how they work.

○ Combining the information about each sphere into the study of Earth as a whole helps scientists gain a more accurate picture of Earth.

# Chapter 16  The Geosphere

Geology

# 16.1 Introduction

The term geosphere refers to the part of Earth that is made of rocks, minerals, and soils. The geosphere extends from the surface of Earth all the way to the very center. Geological activity occurs in the geosphere and includes earthquakes and volcanoes.

Scientists think the geosphere is made of several layers that are different from one another. One way to describe the geosphere is to divide it into three main layers: the crust, the mantle, and the core.

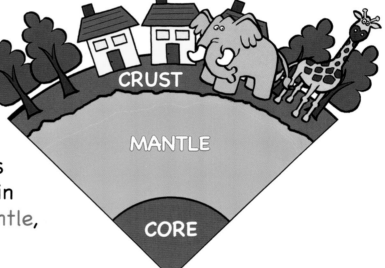

To create a more detailed picture of Earth's layers, geologists often subdivide the main layers of Earth into additional layers. This is helpful when more specific descriptions of the geosphere are needed. Scientists group and name the various layers in different ways according to what will be most helpful to them in studying the geosphere. There is no one right way to list Earth's layers. It just depends on what kinds of questions scientists want to answer.

# 16.2 More About Layers

Although scientists can use different names for the layers of the geosphere, in this book we will use the following names for the layers: the crust, the mantle (divided into the lithosphere, asthenosphere, and mesosphere), and the core (divided into the outer core and the inner core).

The crust is the outermost layer of Earth and is the part of the geosphere that we live on. The crust is hard and is made of rocks, soil, and minerals. The crust makes up mountains, the ocean floor, mesas, river beds, and other features.

Below the crust is the mantle, which is further subdivided into three layers called the lithosphere, asthenosphere, and mesosphere.

The lithosphere lies just below the crust and, like the crust, is a hard, rocky layer. Geologists believe the lithosphere is broken up into huge pieces called plates. It is thought that the lithosphere sits on top of a soft, putty-like layer called the asthenosphere which is made of molten (melted) rock called magma. Heat in the asthenosphere causes the magma in this layer to move. As the magma moves, it carries the plates of the lithosphere along with it, causing earthquakes and volcanoes as the plates shift and push against each other.

Below the asthenosphere is the mesosphere. The mesosphere makes up the largest part of the mantle. Scientists believe that the mesosphere is more solid than the asthenosphere.

Below the mesosphere and at the very center of Earth is the core. The core is divided into the outer core and the inner core. The outer core is thought to be made of liquid rock and metal, and the inner core is thought to be solid. Since it isn't possible to drill to the center of the Earth, geologists don't know exactly what the outer core and the inner core are like, but they can make educated guesses based on the data they collect from experiments.

It's good to keep in mind that scientists sometimes use different groupings and names for the layers of Earth. For example, sometimes the lithosphere and asthenosphere are grouped together and called the upper mantle with the mesosphere being called the lower mantle. And at other times, geologists may group the crust and lithosphere together into a layer they simply call the lithosphere.

## 16.3 Evidence and Guessing

There is much about the geosphere that geologists simply don't know. Because we have not been able to dig below the Earth's crust, we can't get samples of the Earth's interior. This means that some of the conclusions scientists make about how the geosphere works are more like educated guesses.

An educated guess is a guess based on scientific information. When there is enough information to suggest that an educated guess is correct, the guess can become a scientific theory. Sometimes an educated guess is discarded when new evidence suggests that the idea is incorrect. Either way, we gain more understanding of how the geosphere works by looking at evidence, making educated guesses, developing theories, and then discarding theories and guesses when new information challenges old ideas.

For example, as we saw earlier, geologists have found evidence that supports the idea that the lithosphere is divided into plates and earthquakes are caused by the movement of these plates on the soft asthenosphere. Scientists also think that the magma in the asthenosphere can be forced through cracks or thin places in the lithosphere, causing volcanoes to erupt.

There is no way to actually sample the lithosphere or the asthenosphere, so geologists don't know for certain that the lithosphere is hard and the asthenosphere is soft and putty-like. However, they can use advanced tools to gather information, and based on that information they can make an educated guess about what the lithosphere and the asthenosphere are like.

# 16.4 The Geosphere and Other Spheres

The crust is one part of the geosphere that is affected directly by the other spheres, like the atmosphere, the biosphere, and the hydrosphere. The crust is shaped both by the lower layers of Earth where earthquakes and volcanoes begin and by wind, rain, storms, and animals.

For example, a volcano might erupt and create a tall mountain. Over time the mountain may erode and become smaller and smaller because of wind and rain. An earthquake may occur, creating a new passageway for water, and animals might build their homes in the new waterway, creating small ponds or lakes.

The magnetic field that surrounds Earth is believed to be created by the motion of liquid metals in the outer core. If Earth didn't have a core made mostly of metals, we would not have a magnetic field to form the magnetosphere.

The lower layers of the geosphere are not directly affected by the other spheres of the Earth. It doesn't rain on the asthenosphere, and animals can't dig homes in the mesosphere.

## 16.5 Summary

○ The geosphere includes all the rock parts of Earth and extends from the surface of Earth all the way to the very center.

○ The geosphere can be divided into three main layers: crust, mantle, and core. These main layers can be further subdivided into more layers.

○ Geologists can only take samples of the outermost layer of the geosphere (the crust) and have to make educated guesses about the inner layers.

○ The crust is the layer of the geosphere most affected by other spheres.

# Chapter 17   The Air We Breathe

## 17.1 Introduction

Notice what happens when you breathe. Take a deep breath in. What is going into your lungs? Exhale. What comes out?

Air is the name for what we breathe in and what we breathe out. We live on a planet that has the kind of air needed for life. Without the air on Earth, there wouldn't be animals on farms, ponds full of fish, or forests full of trees.

## 17.2 The Atmosphere

The air we breathe exists in the part of the Earth that scientists call the atmosphere. The atmosphere sits just above the Earth's crust and extends for several miles above the surface.

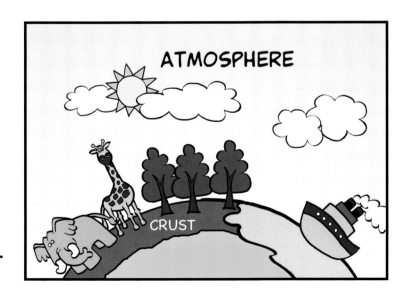

Earth is the only planet in our solar system that has an atmosphere suitable for life as we know it.

Most of the time we don't think too much about the air that surrounds us. We breathe it in and we exhale it out as we go about our day. Some people, though, live in areas where the air is not clean. In some areas of the world, the air contains so much pollution, or small particles, that it is difficult to breathe. Knowing about the air, what it is, and how to keep it clean is important to all living things on Earth.

## 17.3 What Is Air?

You might think most of the air we breathe is oxygen. But it isn't. The air we breathe is a mixture of different gas molecules and water vapor. Air has nitrogen gas, oxygen gas, carbon dioxide gas, a little bit of argon gas, and some water vapor.

Nitrogen gas in the air exists as a molecule with two nitrogen atoms hooked together. When you breathe, nitrogen gas goes inside your lungs and comes out again when you exhale. Your body doesn't use nitrogen gas. It only uses oxygen gas.

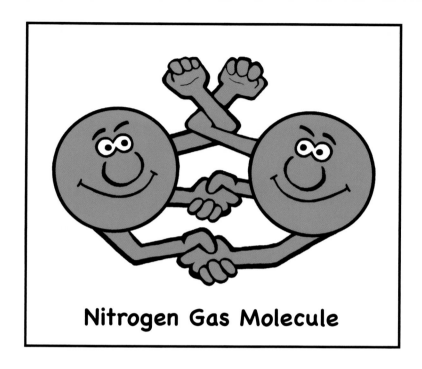

**Nitrogen Gas Molecule**

You have probably heard that you need oxygen to stay alive. In fact, if you hold your breath too long, you will pass out and your body will automatically start breathing again to keep you alive. Oxygen is more important than food or water, and you can't stay alive very long without it.

**Oxygen Gas Molecule**

Oxygen gas is made of two oxygen atoms hooked together. When you breathe in, your lungs expand and oxygen gas goes inside.

Lungs have special cells that absorb oxygen from the air and deliver it to your blood. Your blood has special molecules that then carry the oxygen to the rest of your body. Your body uses the oxygen to process food and give you energy.

After our bodies use the oxygen we have inhaled, they make carbon dioxide gas. Carbon dioxide gas is made of one carbon atom and two oxygen atoms hooked together. When you exhale, you breathe out the carbon dioxide gas.

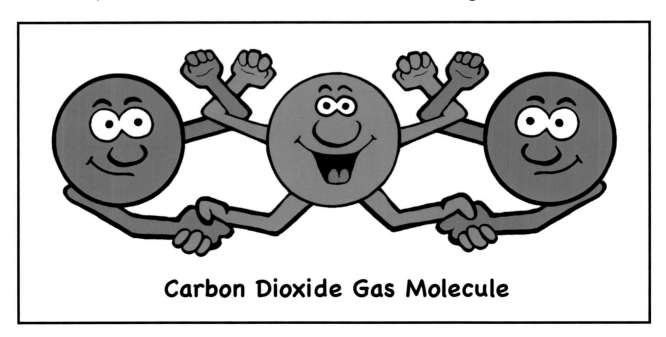

**Carbon Dioxide Gas Molecule**

This works out great because plants use carbon dioxide to make the food that allows them to stay alive and grow. Plants take in carbon dioxide and then put oxygen back into the air. We help plants and plants help us!

## 17.4 Why Doesn't Air Float Away?

You might have wondered if there is oxygen, nitrogen, or carbon dioxide in space. In fact, when astronauts travel outside our atmosphere and into space, they have to wear a special suit so they can have oxygen to breathe.

But what keeps the air we breathe close to the Earth, and why doesn't it just all float away into space? In fact, what keeps you on the Earth, and why don't you float away?

You don't float away for the same reason the air in our atmosphere doesn't float away. Gravity keeps you on the ground and keeps the air we breathe close to the Earth's surface. Gravity is a force that pulls everything near the Earth toward its center. Go ahead and try to jump off the Earth. As soon as you jump up, you will feel Earth's gravity pulling you back down again.

## 17.5 Summary

○ The air we breathe is in the Earth's atmosphere.

○ The air we breathe is made up of nitrogen gas, oxygen gas, carbon dioxide gas, argon gas, and water vapor.

○ Our bodies inhale air, use the oxygen, and then exhale carbon dioxide gas.

○ Gravity keeps the air from floating away into space.

# Chapter 18 Astronomer's Toolbox

Astronomy

# 18.1 Introduction

How can you study objects in space when they are so far away? How can you make discoveries about what other solar systems are like when you can't get on a spaceship and go to them? How can you find out what other planets are like when you can't land on them?

Astronomers depend on a variety of tools to help them visualize the cosmos. New discoveries in astronomy have been made possible by the invention of computers, satellites, and spaceships that can travel far from Earth. Although the study of astronomy is changing quickly as more new tools help astronomers explore space, the invention of a basic tool, the telescope, was the first step in the exploration of space.

# 18.2 Brief History of a Basic Tool

In the 1400s and 1500s when Copernicus was gazing at the night sky, looking up at the stars and wondering about the cosmos, he had to do all of his investigating without the help of a telescope.

Copernicus was smart, and he revolutionized the way we think about the universe by using mathematics to show that the Earth moves around the Sun and that the Sun remains fixed in one location. But without being able to see the details of the Sun and of planets and their moons, Copernicus was limited in what he could explore.

Galileo was exploring the skies, just like Copernicus, but Galileo was born during the time when the telescope was being invented. In the early 1600's Galileo found out about a spyglass invented by a Dutch lens maker named Hans Lippershey. Galileo knew that this spyglass could help him study the cosmos by allowing him see things that were far away in more detail.

Galileo used the ideas that Lippershey had come up with and created his own spyglasses that would eventually become telescopes.

# 18.3 What Is a Telescope?

A telescope is a tool or instrument that helps astronomers see far into the distance. A simple telescope has two lenses connected by a long tube.

One lens is called the eyepiece and is located at one end of the tube. You look through this lens with your eye.

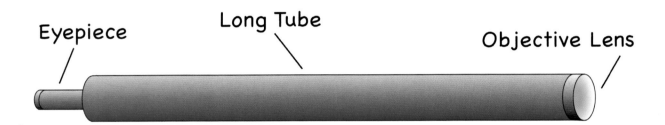

Eyepiece    Long Tube    Objective Lens

The other lens is called the objective lens and is located at the other end of the tube. The objective lens is used to collect light so an object may be viewed.

As light travels through the objective lens and down the tube, it is focused by the eyepiece. In this way the object being viewed becomes magnified, or made to appear larger. The larger the objective lens, the more light can be collected, and the longer the tube, the larger the object will appear.

# 18.4 Early Telescopes

Early telescopes looked very much like the simple telescope described in the previous section. Early telescopes were often made of metal, such as brass or copper, and had two simple lenses, one at either end of a long tube.

Early Telescope
Photo Credit: John Vicari

The body of the metal tube was sometimes attached to a stand. The astronomer could pivot the telescope on its stand, adjusting the direction in which the telescope was pointing.

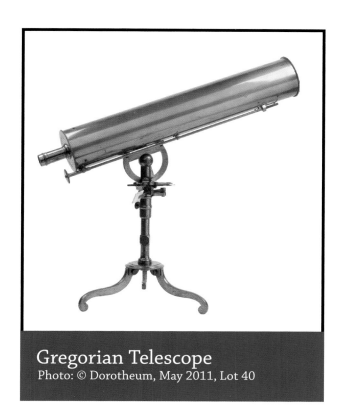

Gregorian Telescope
Photo: © Dorotheum, May 2011, Lot 40

Part of the problem with these early telescopes was that in order to see a faraway object the tube had to be very long. With the invention of the Gregorian telescope and the Newtonian telescope, mirrors were added to the inside of the telescope tube to solve this problem.

In both the Gregorian and Newtonian telescopes, mirrors in the tube are used to focus the light that enters through the objective lens. When the light hits the mirrors, it is bounced from the mirrors into the eyepiece. This design allows astronomers to see distant objects with telescopes that have shorter tubes.

# 18.5 Advanced Telescopes

The telescope has come a long way from the spyglass of Galileo's day. Technological advances have resulted in significant improvements for the modern telescope. Today, astronomers can see not only the planets and their moons in our own solar system but also planets and moons in other solar systems!

A galaxy is a large group of solar systems, stars, and other objects in space. Using modern telescopes, astronomers can now see whole solar systems, not only in Earth's galaxy, but in other galaxies as well!

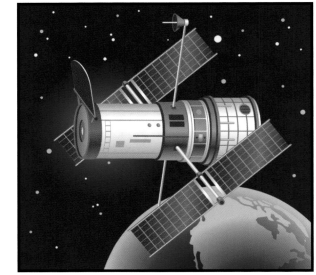

The Hubble Space Telescope is an advanced telescope. As the name suggests, the Hubble Space telescope is actually in space orbiting the Earth. The Hubble Space Telescope was launched into space in 1990 and has produced some of the most amazing images of space we have ever seen.

# 18.6 Summary

- Astronomers explore space by using tools such as telescopes, computers, satellites, and spaceships.

- Galileo modified the spyglass to create a telescope.

- Early telescopes had an objective lens and an eyepiece that were connected by a long tube.

- The Hubble Space Telescope is an advanced telescope that is in space and travels around the Earth.

# Chapter 19  Observing the Constellations

Astronomy

# 19.1 Introduction

No matter where you are on Earth, if you look up to the sky on a clear, dark night, you can see stars. If you are far away from city lights, it looks like the sky is filled with thousands and thousands of stars. There are so many stars that it is difficult to know the name of each star in the sky.

Even without using a telescope, modern satellites, or space probes, we can learn something about the cosmos by observing stars that form constellations. A constellation is a group of stars that together appear to form a shape or image in the sky. By grouping stars into constellations, a lot can be learned about the sky without knowing all the individual stars.

Some common constellations easily observed in the Northern Hemisphere include the Big Dipper and Cassiopeia. Favorite Southern Hemisphere constellations include the Archer and the Whale.

Since Earth is a large sphere, the stars someone can see at the North Pole are different from the stars someone can see at the South Pole. If you are at the equator, over the course of a year you can see all the constellations, but the stars at the North and South Poles will be harder to see.

The constellations change their positions in the sky throughout the night and during the different seasons. This repositioning of the stars is caused by the Earth changing its position in space as it spins on its axis and revolves around the Sun. As the Earth moves, we see the constellations from different angles.

By observing the positions of the constellations in the sky, you can watch the seasons come and go, tell what time of night it is, and determine which direction you are going when traveling on land, sea, or in the air. Knowing the constellations could even help you find your way home if you were taking a trip in outer space!

# 19.2 Northern Hemisphere Constellations

If you live in the Northern Hemisphere there are many constellations you can easily find. A favorite group of stars in the northern sky is called the Big Dipper because its shape looks like a dipper, or ladle. The Big Dipper has 7 stars, three of which form the "handle" and four that form the "bowl" of the dipper. The best time to see The Big Dipper is from February through June.

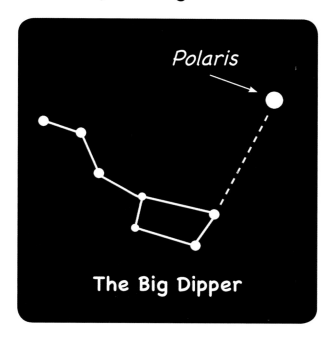

*Polaris*

**The Big Dipper**

The Big Dipper can be used to locate the star Polaris, which is also called the North Star. Polaris can be found by imagining a line going between the two stars located at the end of the bowl of the Big Dipper and extending the line to a lone star that has no other stars nearby. This star is Polaris.

Polaris is above the northernmost point of the Earth. Because it is near enough to true north, it can be used as a navigational marker. If you were on a boat sailing from Maine to England on a clear night, you could use Polaris to keep your boat on track.

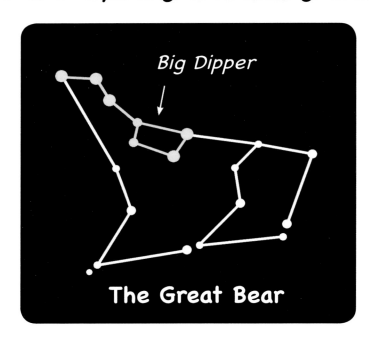

Another interesting constellation to find in the Northern Hemisphere is the Great Bear. The Great Bear includes the Big Dipper. To locate the Great Bear, first find the Big Dipper, and while keeping the Big Dipper in view, expand your gaze to include the three pairs of stars that form the Bear's paws. Once you have these stars and the Big Dipper in view, you can see the rest of the stars that make up the Great Bear. The best time to see the Great Bear is from February through June.

Another favorite constellation is Orion the Hunter. The stars that make up Orion are bright and beautiful which makes it easy to pick out this constellation. A good way to find Orion is to find his belt. Orion's belt is made of three bright stars close together in a straight row. From there you can pick out the shield and raised club. The best time to see Orion is December through March.

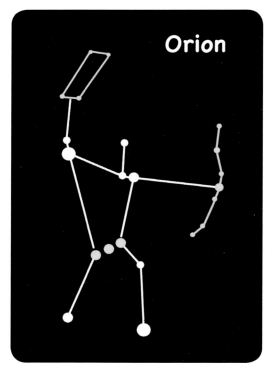

# 19.3 Southern Hemisphere Constellations

If you live in the Southern Hemisphere, there are lots of fun constellations you can find. One of the largest southern constellations is the Whale. The stars that make up the Whale are dim, but because there are fewer stars to observe in this section of the sky, the Whale can be easily seen on a dark night when there is no Moon or city lights.

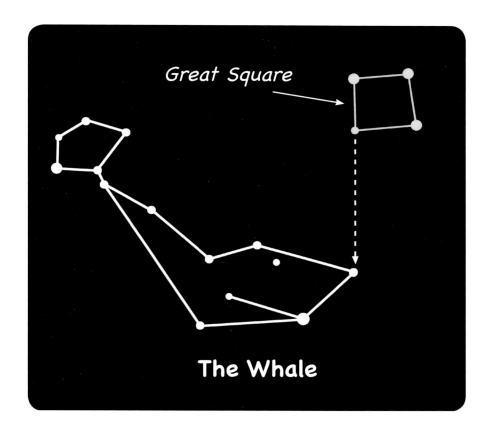

**The Whale**

To find the Whale, first locate the Great Square. As the name suggests, the Great Square is a set of four bright stars that form a square. Once you locate The Great Square, the Whale is easy to spot. Just follow the line made by the two stars on the side of the Great Square until you see a cluster of 4 to 5 stars. These are the stars that make up the head of the Whale. The best time to see the Whale is October through January.

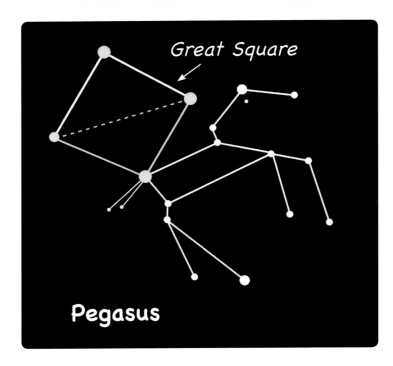

Pegasus

Another favorite constellation in the Southern Hemisphere is Pegasus, the winged horse. Part of the Pegasus constellation includes three of the four stars of the Great Square. These three stars make up the wing of Pegasus which sits on the hind end of the horse. Two little stars near the hind end make up the tail and the head extends in the opposite direction from the tail. The best time of the year to see Pegasus is from August to October.

# 19.4 Using Stars to Navigate

How do you find your way to the grocery store? How do you know which street to take to the park? If you need to go to a friend's house, do you turn to your right, left, or go straight ahead from your front door?

In each of these situations, you are navigating your way from one place to another place. Navigation simply means to make one's way from one location to another. There are several different techniques people use to navigate.

One way to navigate is to use landmarks. If you walk to the grocery store with your parents, you might notice that it is located just across from a park and next to a gas station. The next time you need to go to the grocery store, you can use your knowledge of the park and the gas station as landmarks to guide you to the store. However, if

you were far out to sea where there are no landmarks, how would you find your way home?

This was a problem for early sailors. When traveling along

the coast, they could use landmarks to find their way, but what happened when they traveled far enough out in the ocean that they could no longer see the shore? Early sailors discovered that they could use the stars as a way to navigate across the sea. Using the stars is a great way to find your way, whether you are on land, sea, in an airplane or even in space!

One easy star to use for navigation in the Northern Hemisphere is Polaris. Unlike other stars, Polaris actually stays in the same place in the sky and doesn't appear to move. The north pole of Earth's axis points almost directly at Polaris. If you can find Polaris, you can tell which way is north, and once you locate north, you can find south, east, and west.

In the Southern Hemisphere people use the Southern Cross constellation for navigation. Although Earth's axis at the South Pole doesn't point directly at an individual star, the two stars that form the long part of the constellation can be used to find south.

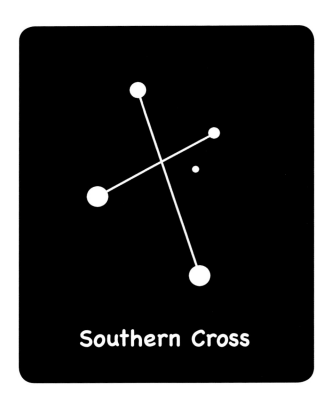

**Southern Cross**

# 19.5 Summary

- A constellation is a group of stars that together form a particular shape.

- Common constellations in the Northern Hemisphere include the Big Dipper, the Great Bear, and Orion.

- Common constellations in the Southern Hemisphere include the Whale and Pegasus, both of which can be located by finding the Great Square.

- Stars can be used to navigate, or find the way, from one location to another.

# Chapter 20 Earth's Neighborhood

Astronomy

# 20.1 Introduction

In our solar system there are two different types of planets. Some of our planetary neighbors are Earth-like, or terrestrial, and some are Jupiter-like, or Jovian. In this chapter we will take a look at where our planetary neighbors "live" in our solar neighborhood.

# 20.2 Our Solar Neighborhood

Most people live in some kind of neighborhood. A neighborhood is an area of town with houses, apartments, a few businesses, and possibly a park.

If you take a walk down the block in your neighborhood, you can see where your neighbors live. Some of your neighbors live close to you. Maybe they live next door and share the same backyard. Other neighbors live farther away, but they may all go to the local grocery store or walk their dog in the local park. We would say that all of the people who live in this particular area of town are part of a neighborhood.

In the same way, planets share a particular area in space. A solar system is made up of a sun and the planets and other objects that travel around that sun.

In our solar system, there are eight planets. All of the planets share the same sun. Some planets are closer to our Sun, and some are farther away, just like the neighbors in your neighborhood.

The closest planet to the Sun and the smallest planet is Mercury. Because Mercury is so close to the Sun, its surface can be very hot. The temperature at noon on Mercury can get up to as much as 425 degrees Celsius (800 degrees Fahrenheit)! But Mercury does not have enough air to hold onto the heat from the Sun. At night the temperature on Mercury can go down to below 18 degrees Celsius (below zero degrees Fahrenheit). So Mercury does not have the right temperatures for plants and animals to be able to live.

The next closet planet to the Sun is Venus. Venus is about twice as far away from the Sun as Mercury. However, even though Venus is farther away from the Sun than Mercury is, Venus is actually hotter! Venus has lots of carbon dioxide in the air. This heats up the surface and holds the heat so

Venus is hot all the time. The surface of Venus can reach over 460 degrees Celsius (860 degrees Fahrenheit). Venus is much too hot to support plant and animal life.

 The next closest planet to the Sun is Earth. Earth is close enough to the Sun to have enough heat for life to exist, but not so close that it is too hot for living things. Earth is the only planet in our solar system that supports plant and animal life.

Mars sits farther away from the Sun than Earth does. Mars is much colder than Earth because it is farther away from the Sun. However, Mars is almost close enough to the Sun to support life.

Mercury, Venus, Earth, and Mars make up the inner solar system, or inner neighborhood. From an astronomer's perspective, all of these planets are relatively close to each other.

Much farther out are the four planets in the outer solar system. Jupiter is the first planet in the outer solar system. Jupiter is more than five times farther away from the Sun than Earth is.

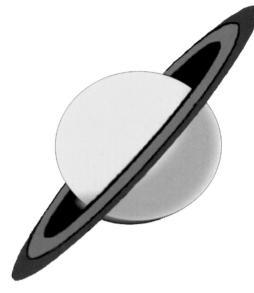

Saturn is even farther away from the Sun than Jupiter is. Saturn is the second planet in the outer solar system.

Uranus and Neptune are the last two planets in the outer solar system.

Neptune is almost 30 times as far away from the Sun as Earth is. Jupiter, Saturn, Uranus, and Neptune are all much too cold to support plant and animal life.

# 20.3 Orbits

The planets don't just sit in one spot, but move in a nearly circular orbit around the Sun. An orbit is a particular path, like a road, that a planet follows.

Each planet stays in its orbit at its particular distance away from the Sun. Planets don't cross other planetary orbits or ever bump into each other.

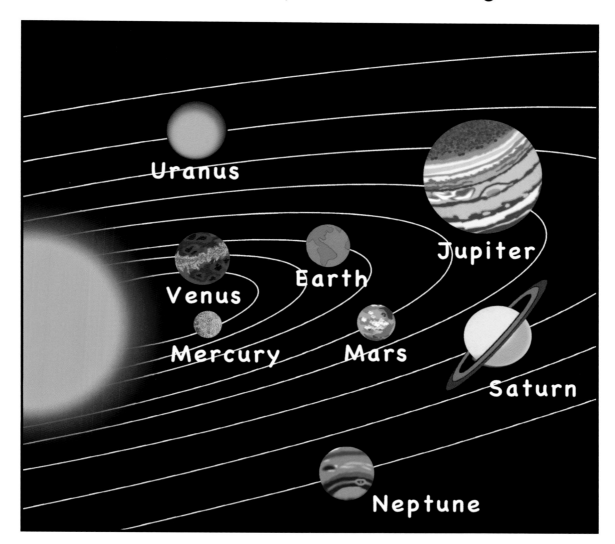

Each planet takes a certain number of days to orbit the Sun. This is called a planetary year. Mercury orbits the Sun faster than does any other planet. It only takes 88 days for Mercury to complete one orbit. So one year on Mercury is only 88 days.

It takes Venus a little longer than Mercury to orbit the Sun, but not as long as it takes Earth. Venus orbits the Sun in 225 days, and Earth orbits the Sun in 365 days. The length of our calendar year is 365 days.

It takes Mars 687 days to orbit the Sun, and it takes Jupiter almost 12 Earth years to complete one planetary year!

Saturn takes almost 30 Earth years to orbit the Sun, and Uranus orbits the Sun in 84 Earth years. If you lived on Neptune you would need 165 Earth years just to get around the Sun once!

| Planet | Number of Days for One Orbit of the Sun |
|---|---|
| Mercury | 88 |
| Venus | 225 |
| Earth | 365 |
| Mars | 687 |
| Jupiter | 4,332 |
| Saturn | 10,760 |
| Uranus | 30,700 |
| Neptune | 60,200 |

# 20.4 Why Is Earth Special?

Of all the planets in our solar system, only Earth is the right distance away from the Sun, with the right combination of water, oxygen, minerals, and soils to support plant and animal life. Earth has just the right conditions for plant and animal life to exist.

Earth has many unique features that make it just right for plant and animal life. If Earth were closer to the Sun, it

would be too hot for life. If Earth were farther away from the Sun, it would be too cold for life. If Earth's atmosphere had too much gas, like Venus does, it would cause the Earth's surface to heat up and would make it too hot.

Earth is special in this way. There is no other planet in our solar system that can support plant and animal life. And so far, no other planet in the universe has been found that supports plant and animal life. Earth has just the right temperature, is just the right distance from the Sun, and is made of just the right materials for plant and animal life to exist!

# 20.5 Summary

- We live together with other planets in a planetary neighborhood called the solar system.

- All of the planets in our solar system share the same sun.

- Mercury is closest to the Sun, followed by Venus, Earth, Mars, Jupiter, Saturn, Uranus, and Neptune.

- Each planet rotates around the Sun in an orbit.

- Each planet takes a different number of days to complete one orbit around the Sun. The number of days it takes a planet to orbit the Sun once is called a planetary year. Our planetary year is 365 days.

# Chapter 21 Beyond the Neighborhood

Astronomy

# 21.1 Introduction

In Chapter 20 we looked at our planetary neighborhood called the solar system. We saw how the eight planets orbit the Sun and why Earth is the only planet in our solar system that can support plant and animal life.

But what about other solar systems? What lies beyond our neighborhood? Are there other neighborhoods with suns like ours and planets like ours that support plant and animal life?

# 21.2 Nearest Star

If you look up into the sky on a dark, clear night, you can see lots of stars. On a moonless night, far away from the city lights, you might be able to see 2,000 stars or more.

The closest star to our Earth is a star called Proxima Centauri. Proxima Centauri is actually part of a three-star system. The two other stars in this system are called Alpha Centauri A and Alpha Centauri B. Alpha Centauri A, Alpha Centauri B, and Proxima Centauri orbit each other.

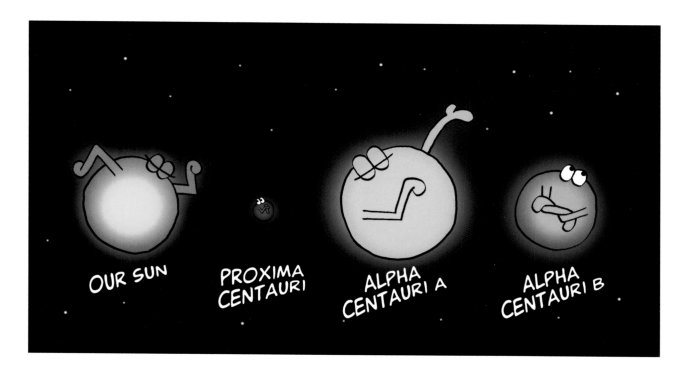

Proxima Centauri is smaller and cooler than our Sun and is red in color. Even though Proxima Centauri is the closest star to our Sun, it is not bright enough to be seen without a telescope.

# 21.3 Brightest Star

The brightest star we can see in the sky is called Sirius. Sirius is farther away than Proxima Centauri but is brighter. The brightness of a star does not depend on how close it is, but on how much light the star makes.

One way to think about how much light a star makes is to look at the difference between a candle and a flashlight. A candle will light up or illuminate an area of a meter or so (a few feet) around it, but a flashlight can illuminate several meters (yards). A flashlight puts out more energy than a candle and as a result can illuminate a much longer distance.

If you were to look at a candle and a flashlight from several meters (yards) away, the flashlight would look brighter. If you moved the flashlight a few meters (yards) farther away than the candle, it would still look brighter.

In the same way, Sirius is a brighter star than Proxima Centauri even though it is farther away.

# 21.4 Biggest Star

The biggest star is not necessarily the closest star or the brightest star. The biggest star we can see from Earth is called VY Canis Majoris or VY CMa.

VY CMa is about 2,000 times larger than our Sun. If VY CMa were in our solar system replacing our Sun, it would extend beyond the orbit of Saturn!

# 21.5 Stars With Planets

Scientists think that most stars have planets orbiting them.

It is very difficult for astronomers to see the planets in other solar systems directly. Planets are very dim because they don't produce their own light like suns do. However, astronomers can use other techniques to figure out if stars have planets orbiting them. One technique is to use physics to determine if a star is wobbling. As planets orbit a sun, their gravity pulls on the sun, causing it to wobble. Astronomers can study a sun's wobble to determine if one or more planets might exist in orbit around the sun.

Many planets in other solar systems have been found, but so far none of them appear to be like Earth. In order for a planet to be able support plant and animal life, the planet would need to be close to a sun. However, if it were too close, the planet would be too hot. If the planet were too far away from the sun, it would be too cold. Also, the sun would have to be large enough to produce enough energy for plants and animals to use.

Scientists continue to search for life on other planets. So far, Earth is the only planet that we know supports plant and animal life.

## 21.6 Summary

- Our nearest neighboring star is Proxima Centauri.

- The brightest star is Sirius.

- The largest star is VY Canis Majoris (VY CMa).

- So far, Earth is the only planet we know of that supports plant and animal life.

# Chapter 22  Putting It All Together

Conclusion

# 22.1 Tools and Science

In this book you learned about the many tools scientists use to study the world around us. The tools scientists use vary depending on what is being studied. Also, in each of the core subjects of chemistry, biology, physics, geology, and astronomy, there are a few basic tools and a greater number of advanced tools.

# 22.2 Sharing Tools

Scientists often share their tools with other scientists who are studying different core subjects. For example, a chemist may use some of the same tools as a biologist, and a biologist may use some of the same tools as a chemist. For instance, while

performing an experiment to study small molecules in a cell, a biologist might need to use a beaker, a basic tool commonly used by chemists.

A chemist studying the atoms in a geode might need to use a geologist's rock hammer to break the geode open. Or an astronomer looking for life on other objects in space might use a biologist's microscope to examine moon rocks to look for tiny archaea or bacteria.

# 22.3 Working Together

Most scientists specialize in a specific subject area, but in many research labs scientists who specialize in different subjects work together. It is not uncommon to see chemists working side-by-side with biologists and physicists to solve a specific scientific problem.

Teams of scientists working together to solve problems is a great way to perform experiments. Many problems need to be examined from different viewpoints in order to find a solution. Chemists may think of solving problems in ways that are different from biologists. Also, because there is so much scientific information that has been discovered and studied, no one scientist can learn everything there is to know about science. Therefore, having a group of scientists collaborate (work together) on a project is the best way to learn.

## 22.4 Summary

- Scientists who study chemistry, biology, physics, geology, and astronomy use both basic and advanced tools.

- Scientists who specialize in a core subject learn how to use tools specific to their subject.

- Scientists share tools with each other.

- Scientists from different core subject areas work in groups and collaborate on projects.

# More REAL SCIENCE-4-KIDS Books
## by Rebecca W. Keller, PhD

**Building Blocks Series** yearlong study program — each Student Textbook has accompanying Laboratory Notebook, Teacher's Manual, Lesson Plan, Study Notebook, Quizzes, and Graphics Package

Exploring the Building Blocks of Science Book K (Activity Book)
Exploring the Building Blocks of Science Book 1
Exploring the Building Blocks of Science Book 2
Exploring the Building Blocks of Science Book 3
Exploring the Building Blocks of Science Book 4
Exploring the Building Blocks of Science Book 5
Exploring the Building Blocks of Science Book 6
Exploring the Building Blocks of Science Book 7
Exploring the Building Blocks of Science Book 8

**Focus Series** unit study program — each title has a Student Textbook with accompanying Laboratory Notebook, Teacher's Manual, Lesson Plan, Study Notebook, Quizzes, and Graphics Package

Focus On Elementary Chemistry
Focus On Elementary Biology
Focus On Elementary Physics
Focus On Elementary Geology
Focus On Elementary Astronomy

Focus On Middle School Chemistry
Focus On Middle School Biology
Focus On Middle School Physics
Focus On Middle School Geology
Focus On Middle School Astronomy

Focus On High School Chemistry

## Super Simple Science Experiments

21 Super Simple Chemistry Experiments
21 Super Simple Biology Experiments
21 Super Simple Physics Experiments
21 Super Simple Geology Experiments
21 Super Simple Astronomy Experiments
101 Super Simple Science Experiments

**Note:** A few titles may still be in production.

## Gravitas Publications Inc.
www.gravitaspublications.com
www.realscience4kids.com